Kaye Pyke's

ELEGANT EMBROIDERY

KAYE PYKE
and
LYNNE LANDY

Photography by
Neil Lorimer

Illustrations by
Patsy Blair

ALLEN & UNWIN

ACKNOWLEDGEMENTS

We would like to thank the following people for their assistance in the production of this book: MCM Fine Linens, Boyac and Redelman & Son in Melbourne for the loan of linen and fabric for photography. Julie Murray for location shots in her home. Sue Dickens and Robyn MacDonald for embroidering some of the projects in this book. Leslie Thrum for her fine needlework and continued support. Anne Stowers for making up all the cushions. Neil Lorimer and Patsy Blair for their enthusiasm and dedication. Mark Davis for his design work and attention to detail, and Julie Gibbs of Allen & Unwin for her enthusiasm and professional advice.

© 1991 Kaye Pyke and Lynne Landy

Illustrations by Patsy Blair
Photographs by Neil Lorimer
Designed by Mark Davis, text-art

First published in 1991
This paperback edition first published 1995

Allen & Unwin Pty Ltd
9 Atchison Street
St Leonards NSW 2065, Australia

National Library of Australia
cataloguing-in-publication data

    Pyke, Kaye, 1943—
      Kaye Pyke's elegant embroidery
      ISBN 1 86373 876 2 (pbk).

      1. Embroidery - Patterns. I. Landy, Lynne. II. Title.
      III. Title: Elegant Embroidery.

746.44041

Printed in Hong Kong by Dah Hua
10 9 8 7 6 5 4 3 2 1

Cover picture features the Gold Moiré Cushion with Corded Edge and all Ribbon Embroidery.

CONTENTS

INTRODUCTION

Embroidery in the 1990s has a new look and a new purpose. The very word embroidery conjures up Victorian ladies whiling away the hours making cross-stitch samplers, or war-time wives disguising austere fabrics with embroidered flowers.

Embroidery is about to shed its dowdy image! This book introduces needlework for a new age; sophisticated stitchery with panache that's simple to do, satisfying to finish and stunning to look at. It can be subtle or bold, combine ribbons with threads, silks with wools, mix textures and colours, but it need not be difficult or complicated. No experience is necessary!

There is a world-wide resurgence in handcrafts. Knitting and stitching exhibitions are attracting record crowds everywhere. British designer Kaffe Fassett led the way and has shown with his books, videos and international exhibitions, how exciting and sophisticated colourful yarns can be when used for knitting or needlepoint. Classes in needlepoint, patchwork, appliqué and embroidery are springing up everywhere as we rediscover the pleasure and satisfaction of sewing and stitching.

After a decade of consumption and expenditure we are seeing a return to 'old-world' values; the era of the 'throwaway' society is passing and we are looking for products that will last, that can be handed on to our children and grandchildren. If we can make our own 'heirlooms' then so much the better.

In this decade the home is becoming an important focus. Interior decoration has a much greater emphasis and do-it-yourself techniques that have style are booming. The current fashion for decorative

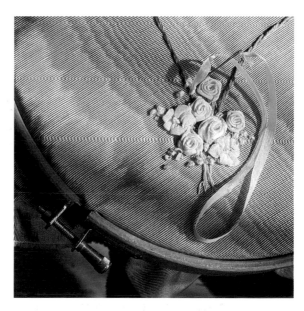

This pastel-coloured silk embroidery on moiré taffeta employs an embroidery frame to keep the fabric taut.

paint finishes such as stencilling and marbling is a good example of a traditional craft that is enjoying a renaissance in the 90s. The current mood in interior design calls for regal colours, rich layers of texture, fabrics with sheen and pattern, tassle and braid trims—a romanticism and luxury that is comfortable to live with. Everyone's home, be it a penthouse or bungalow, can become a castle. This trend for ornate decoration is the perfect vehicle for sophisticated embroidery, yet embroidery that is very simple to do.

Embroidery is in fashion again too—trimming jeans, edging shirt collars and bringing a special femininity to lingerie.

In this book we show you how to start with the simplest project and develop techniques and stitches which result in beautiful handmade pieces to be proud of. The stitches are simple, the materials often inexpensive yet the results are very satisfying and add new glamour to the home and make very personal gifts.

Embroidery has a calming effect. It can be done anywhere—on a plane, in a train or just sitting at the fireside. It is an inexpensive hobby and after initial instruction, your own individual creativity comes into play to produce original pieces. We feel that it is time for a book that shares our excitement about these new design ideas and techniques—but be warned, once you start stitching, you won't stop!

ABOUT KAYE PYKE

KAYE Pyke has a coterie of followers in Melbourne who appreciate her artistry and great sense of style. They have become embroidery enthusiasts as a result of attending one of her classes or are clients who regularly visit her decorating boutique in Port Melbourne. Kaye's students, who often become friends, know that they have been introduced to a range of skills that taps into their own creativity. Once the basic stitches and design techniques have been mastered, the design ideas are limitless.

Kaye is often surprised and delighted at the skilful pieces of work her students create, and some of their ideas have been incorporated into this book. Her students come from all walks of life—working women who need embroidery as as antidote to an overfull and stressed life, women seeking additional hobbies and those looking for a new outlet for their creative skills. Occasionally two generations attend; mothers and daughters both sharing in the excitement of a new creative pastime.

Kaye started stitching a long time ago. Married and caring for her first child, she had time on her hands at home and so started stitching tapestries. She quickly became bored with repeatedly using the same stitch, so with an overflowing basket of tapestry wool, she decided to experiment and using a remnant of calico, embroidered her first posy. She has never attended a class, is entirely self taught, and perhaps that is why her designs are so free-flowing and full of artistry. Friends saw and admired her embroidered designs on calico and started placing orders for cushions. Soon they wanted to embroider too, and so the classes began with just a few friends at a time, in her sitting room.

At the same time, Georges, a prestigious department store in Melbourne, placed orders for cushions and her career in the decorating business was on its way. Since those early days, Kaye has experimented with yarns and fabrics, increasing her own skills and the designs she makes. Following the 'calico' phase, she started using damask as a base cloth, enjoying the heavier material with its figured patterns. She embroidered white-on-white designs for a range of damask pillows of all shapes and sizes, usually trimmed with lace and ruffles.

Designs on moiré taffeta, silk and velvet followed and Kaye developed techniques for embroidering with ribbons and incorporating ribbon roses. Her embroidery design repertoire today is exciting and varied and she is constantly developing new ideas and themes.

This book not only gives precise instructions on how to do simple embroidery stitches and create a wide range of items, but also suggests how to use embroidered items in the home. Kaye has concentrated in her classes on embroidered pieces that can be put to good use in a home setting, and not stored away in a cupboard. At the beginning of each section, Kaye gives decorating hints which we hope will enable readers to enjoy their handiwork in an appropriate setting.

A group of enthusiastic students enjoy one of Kaye Pyke's embroidery classes.

The rich interior of Kaye Pyke's Port Melbourne decorating boutique reflects her stylish approach.

GETTING STARTED

FABRICS

CALICO

Calico is one of the most underrated fabrics. Its homespun quality and low cost make it ideal for decorating with a lot of style but with a low budget. Use it for ruched balloon blinds, slip covers and of course, for embroidered cushions. It is the perfect fabric for the first time embroiderer, as it is inexpensive, hard to ruin and easy to handle—the fabric is firm and doesn't shift. Try to find a pre-shrunk calico fabric, as it can shrink when washed. However if you are doing wool embroidery, then it is always better to dry-clean the finished item when necessary, as some wool yarns can run during washing.

DAMASK

White or cream damask is the next fabric we use in this book. The white-on-white pillows are simple to do but extremely effective, particularly in a bedroom setting. Small initialled pillows are an ideal wedding or baby gift. Damask fabrics are now available in a range of colours which open up a whole new horizon of embroidery possibilities, including jewel-coloured tablecloths and napkins, or pillows that are trimmed with braids and tassles. Watch out for old damask tablecloths in antique shops or garage sales—they have stains or holes in places, but might yield enough fabric for a small pillow.

SATINS AND SILKS

Never use poor quality fabrics for embroidery. Always use real silk if possible—it is not worth the effort of putting hours of work into embroidery on cheap fabrics. Search the remnant tables in fabric stores—there is often small metreage of fine fabrics available and you can build up a 'library' of fabrics that will become a vital resource. Keep colour swatches of your home colour schemes in your wallet, so when you see a bargain, you can check for colour matching and blending.

As your embroidery skills increase, you will be using combinations of fabrics, so be on the look-out for velvets, cords, moiré taffeta and small quantities of cordings, braids and tassles. You will develop the skill of mixing fabrics together—moiré with silk, velvet with cord, and so on. Heavier fabrics need heavy fringing, finer fabrics more delicate trims.

Finding braids and tassles in the right colours can be difficult—so if you are planning such a project, always buy the tassles first, and coordinate your fabrics around the tassle colouring.

YARN

THERE are two brands of tapestry wool used for the projects shown in this book, Paterna wool yarn from the USA and Appletons, from England. The Paternayan Persian yarn is 100% virgin wool, has a soft lustre and is available in a wonderful range of colours. It is a three ply yarn, which means that it can be separated into single strands when required. The Appletons yarns are very fine and are used for delicate embroidery. The colour range is excellent and they are ideal for use when the blending of two shades together is necessary.

The cotton yarns used are the DMC range, made in England. The colour range is extensive and the quality excellent.

Pure silk ribbons have been used for all the ribbon embroidery. There are synthetic ribbons available which are less expensive, but the silk ribbon is more pliable and you can do more with it.

NEEDLES

Chenille needles have been used for almost all the embroidery in this book. It is a needle with a very large eye and a sharp point. They are sold in a pack, with sizes ranging from 18-24. For ribbon embroidery the size 24 Chenille needle is used. For finer embroidery, try the size 9 embroidery needle by Birch.

GENERAL HINTS

1. Whether to use an embroidery frame is a personal choice. If you find that you have a tendency to pull

the work too tight, then try using a frame. You only need a small frame for any of the projects illustrated in this book.

2. Never worry about the back of your work. Mostly we break all those old-fashioned rules about not using knots and finishing off neatly. No one is ever going to check the back; it will either be inside a cushion or a picture frame. It is far more important to enjoy your stitching.

3. Don't worry about making mistakes—you can always go back and turn that error into an interesting flower! Occasionally the shape may look a little strange but it can easily be balanced out with a little additional stitching.

4. Try always to keep your work loose. Each motif has more texture and stands out better in the finished project.

5. Don't be afraid of colour! Experiment!

6. To thread the needle, fold yarn over at the top, squash it flat and push it through the eye of the needle.

7. When using wool yarns double, instead of using two strands together and threading them both through the needle, thread one strand through, pull it down to join the start and knot, so you have a double thread. This method gives a better texture in the finished work.

8. It is good to have several projects going at the same time. Don't feel that you have to finish one project before starting another. Sometimes you get stuck with a particular piece of work and moving on to something else can help. If something is not working, never put it away completely. You will find that in a few days or weeks, you will be able to see where you have gone wrong, and return to it with renewed enthusiam.

9. Never rush embroidery. Take it easy, relax and enjoy it. If you try to work too quickly, you will make mistakes and become very frustrated. It is intended to be a relaxing pastime—allow it to be just that.

COLOUR

A T Kaye's embroidery classes her first lesson consists of teaching the basic stitches using wool embroidery in a garland design, shown on page 19. The very first step is to select a range of several colours from the basket of tapestry wools. Time and time again she finds that her students are afraid to choose their colours. 'I don't know where to start,' they say. 'What do you think? Should I choose bright shades or pastels?' Her advice is always the same: 'Choose the colours you like, use your own instincts'. They then follow her advice—and the garland made by each student is completely different. Don't be afraid of colour. Your selection will reflect your own personality and you will find that as your design sense grows, you will become more adventurous and develop a better colour sense.

When you start to enjoy embroidery you look at everything around you through new eyes. Nature suddenly becomes a souce of design inspiration, flower colours have new meaning. There are no rules when it comes to colour in nature—flower shades often clash, but look marvellous together and the same applies to embroidery design—consider red and hot pink together, purple and green, lilac and cream. There are no set rules. Tone-on-tone colourings can also look grand—a pillow worked entirely in shades of cream or white, or different shades of blues.

Colour variations can also be introduced into a design by using two strands of wool in different shades in one needle.

A rich palette of embroidery wools, ribbons, silks and needles—the simple tools used for all of Kaye Pyke's designs.

COLOUR

Here are five examples of colour combinations that look great in the garland or posy design or any other wool embroidery. The colour schemes could also be applied to embroidery designs using cotton thread.

1. Mid-pastel scheme: Paternayan Persian Yarns: 604, 614, 622, 704, 344, 506, 523, 948, 947 and 261.
2. Spring floral colour scheme: Paternayan Persian Yarns: 604, 603, 963, 964, 948, 322, 324, 333 and 714.
3. Palette of bright colours: Paternayan Persian Yarns: 610, 651, 650, 541, 341, 710, 352, 311 and 841.
4. Blue and gold shades: Paternayan Persian Yarns: 642, 644, 562, 344, 553, 552, 556, 703, 702 and 735.
5. Green and gold shades: Paternayan Persian Yarns: 642, 644, 884, 886, 875, 727, 701, 735, 703 and 261.

Colour variations can also be introduced by using two strands of wool in different shades in one needle. Sometimes the instructions suggest 'overstitching' one part of a design to give it extra fullness and texture. The skill is in knowing when added texture is needed and when extra stitching would make the design look heavy or clumsy—and this skill develops with experience.

STITCH GLOSSARY I

E VERY project in this book stems from the six basic stitches detailed below. The same stitches are used whether you are working with wool yarns, cotton threads or ribbons.

STRAIGHT STITCH

The most fundamental stitch of all—taking the needle in and out of the fabric over a short space.
Daisy: Straight stitches are placed in a circle to resemble a simple flower.
Leaves: Also made using the straight stitch, with

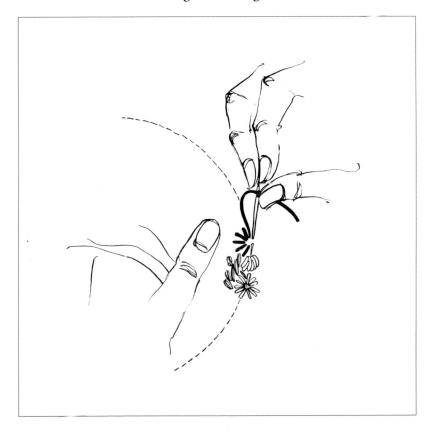

Making a daisy

three stitches comprising one long central stitch, and a short stitch on either side.

Flowerbuds: Made using the same method on a smaller scale, with a central straight stitch and two short straight stitches on either side. Sometimes, for texture, the central stitch is overstitched again.

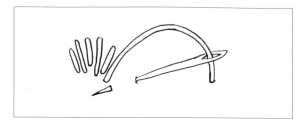

Straight stitch

STEM STITCH

This stitch is used for stems of flowers and borders. Put the needle into the fabric and make a short stitch, bringing the needle back into the tip of the last stitch, giving an overlapping effect.

When using this for a border outline, follow the circle or oval outline with the same method.

Stalks in a posy: Start the stalk by taking a stitch into the base of each flower, making it look as natural as possible. Always use a single thread for stalks, but sometimes overstitching is necessary to achieve a textured or raised look.

Double chain: This is two lines of stem stitch stitched around an outline in the opposite direction to give a chain effect.

Straight stitch—bud flower   *Straight stitch—leaves*

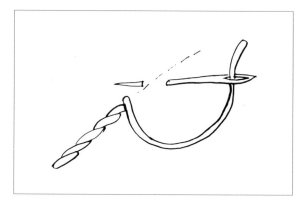

Stem stitch

SATIN STITCH

The most important part of successful satin stitch is keeping the stitches even and loose. Tight stitching makes the fabric pucker and spoils the whole effect. Satin stitch is straight stitch used over and over again. In this book it is used mainly for filling in an outline for bow or ribbon effects.

Double chain stitch

FRENCH KNOT

Bring the needle through the fabric from the back of the work and pull through. Make a tiny stitch at the base of the thread and wind the thread around the needle once or twice (depending on the size of the knot required) and pull through slowly, making sure that the threads around the needle are even and firm. Take the needle to the back again and fasten off.

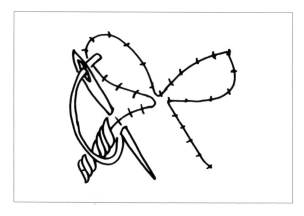

Satin stitch—bow detail

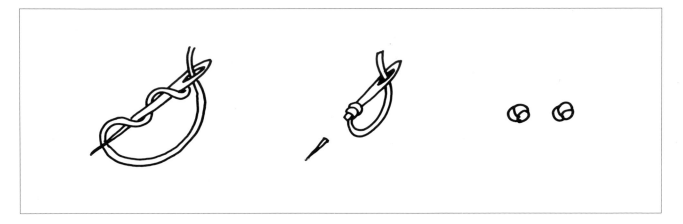

French knot

BULLION ROSE

This is basically the same stitch as the French knot, but the thread is wound around the needle up to 13 times. Pull the thread through slowly, pushing the knots down the needle to be placed evenly on the work. Repeat this method several times, either making the textured knots lie straight, or in a curved or circular manner. This is one of the most difficult stitches and does take quite a bit of practice. Do not despair if it doesn't work for you the first time—keep practising!

ROSETTE STITCH

This is a miniature stem stitch, but used in an ever-decreasing circle. Starting on the outside of a circle shape, make small stem stitches, working around and around in an inwards direction. To finish off the centre, loop the thread around the needle (as in a French knot) and take the thread to the back of the work and fasten off.

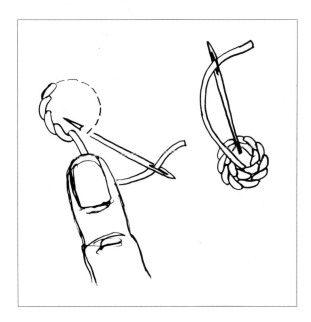

Rosette stitch

Making a bullion rose

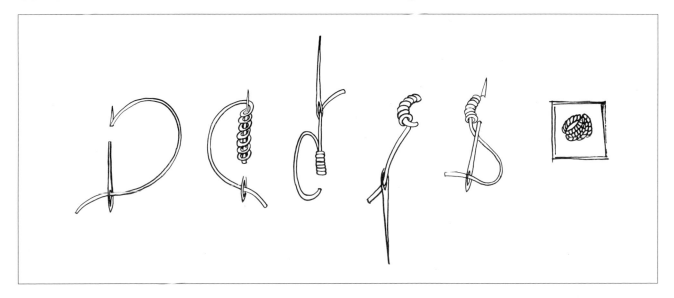

STITCH GLOSSARY II

RIBBON ROSES

To make ribbon roses, always use double sided satin ribbon. It can be from 5mm ($^1/_4$in) to 1cm ($^1/_2$in) wide, depending on the effect that you want.

For a small rose, take a piece of ribbon 25cm (10in) long, making sure that the ribbon has been cut off neatly, with a straight edge. Starting from the end of the ribbon, fold it in, over and over three to four times, then sew at one end with needle and matching cotton. With the ribbon in your right hand, fold the ribbon over away from you on the diagonal, then turn it halfway around the bud rose, once again securing with stitches at the base.

Repeat this over and over until all the ribbon has been used and you have a ribbon rose. Stitch the final fold under the work, making sure it looks neat and is very secure. Making ribbon roses is for the patient—they are very fiddly to make, but the end result is well worth your time and effort. The main thing always to remember, is to secure each fold as you make the rose. If you just wind around the petals without stitching, the rose will fall apart when you place it on your work.

PEONY ROSES

Make the ribbon rose as detailed above, and use this as the centre of the flower. Cut several short lengths of ribbon between 4-6cm (2-3in) long (the number of pieces depends on the size of the rose). Each additional petal is made separately so gather each piece of ribbon with short running stitches. Stitch

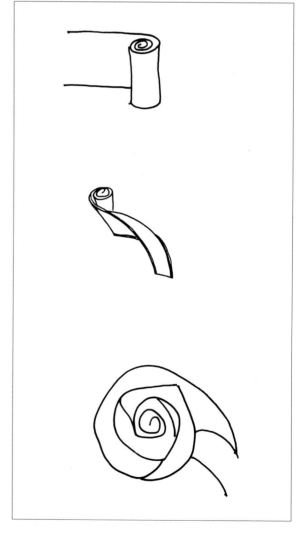

Ribbon rose

each petal individually around the centre of the rose; they do not all have to be the same size. Add as many petals as you need for the size of the rose in the design. When the rose is complete, stitch it on to the fabric, making sure that the stitches are hidden.

When making peony roses, it is most important to use ribbons in slightly different shades of colour in order to achieve the right effect—use paler ribbons for the centre of the flowers and darker ribbons for the outer petals.

ROSEBUDS

Cut a short length of ribbon. Fold this in half, so that it forms a loop. Cut it off square at the base of the loop. Sew it securely with matching cotton and wind around the base to gather it in. Fold the stitched base upward so that it forms padding (ie the rosebud) inside the loop. Stitch firmly and attach it to the work.

RIBBON LEAVES

Make these in the same way as the rosebuds, but without the padding. Add them to the flower, hiding the base under the flower so to appear as a leaf.

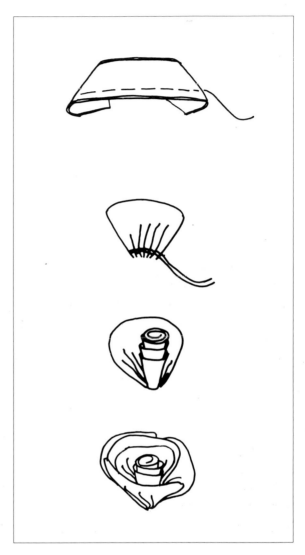

Constructing a peony rose

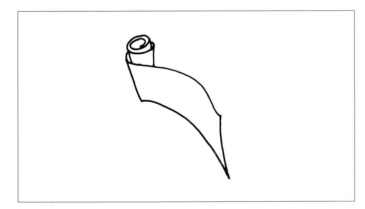

Ribbon rosebud

Ribbon leaves

STITCH GLOSSARY III

RIBBON EMBROIDERY

Always use one hundred per cent silk ribbons for ribbon embroidery. There are other synthetic ribbons available but the pure silk is much easier to work with, and the results are always pleasing. The silk ribbons are a standard 2mm ($^1/_8$in) wide.

Always use short lengths of ribbon, approximately 28cm (11in) long, to avoid tangling and wear and tear on the ribbon.

When threading the needle, it is always best to knot the end of the ribbon, by putting the ribbon through the needle, and then piercing the end of the ribbon with the needle. Pull the needle through, forming a knot. This prevents you losing the ribbon as you work.

You will find that the ribbon tends to twist as you sew. To avoid this, always straighten the ribbon as you pull it through before taking the next stitch. Using short lengths of ribbon helps with this problem. The stitches used for all the projects in this book are identical to the basic stitches illustrated in Stitch Glossary I.

RIBBON DAISY

The method is similar to that of the daisy in Stitch Glossary I, but instead of pulling the ribbon through, you allow the ribbon to sit loosely on the top of the fabric, making a soft loop.

Ribbon daisy

♡ BEGINNERS PLEASE !

These wool-embroidered calico cushions illustrate the colourful impact of simple designs in a country setting.

ECORATING on a budget can be fun. All you need is a good eye and imagination, time for browsing and bargaining, and the vision of how you would like your home to look.

Choose a theme—perhaps a country look or a French provincial mood and build a colour scheme around this. The time taken to plan carefully is always time well spent.

Build up a file of magazine clippings of rooms that you love, and develop your decorating theme from these. Carry a 'colour file' with you at all times with paint samples and fabric swatches so that when you spot a bargain piece of furniture or a fabric remnant, you can check that the colours will blend or complement.

Browse in opportunity shops, auction rooms and country clearing sales for furniture bargains and accessories. If you find a lamp that is broken, or a chair that needs fixing, it may still be worth buying second-hand as there are plenty of places which specialise in repair work. Buying new doesn't always mean buying well—sometimes older pieces of furniture are better made, and can look a million dollars with new upholstery or loose covers.

If you are starting from scratch, think about finding second-hand furniture that can be given a facelift with calico loose covers, which look smart and are easily laundered. Your embroidered cushions will add the personal touch and calico festoon blinds or curtains, using the same fabric but in generous quantities, add the look of luxury that belies the small budget.

Calico can come to the rescue in an apartment that has damaged walls and shabby paintwork. Take two curtain rods the length of the wall, then tightly gather the calico on to the top and bottom rods, making a shirred effect. These calico panels can be attached to the walls in the corner of the room and will provide an attractive and inexpensive disguise. This casual decor could have inexpensive coir matting on the floor, and this too can sometimes be purchased in job lots at auction. Old furniture that has seen better days will benefit from a new coat of paint, sometimes with hand-painted flowers or using a stencil kit.

If you are decorating on a tight budget, don't expect to achieve too much in a hurry—that is the way expensive mistakes are made. Take your time and enjoy each new purchase as you find it. The enjoyment you get from gradually reaching your decorating goals is long-lasting and satisfying.

GARLAND PILLOW

MATERIALS

2m (2$^1/_4$yds) calico (this amount allows for a
full frill and the back of the cushion)
Chenille needle, size 20
Paternayan Persian yarns, colours as follows:

blue 341	purple 311
pink 352	strawberry red 902
yellow 710	green 610
deep pink 351	gold 751

INSTRUCTIONS

All the stitches used in this garland are illustrated in
Stitch Glossary I. All stitches use a single strand of
yarn. If a thicker effect is needed in places, overstitch
again.

1. Cut out a calico square 36cm (14in) in diameter.
2. Draw a circle 15cm (6in) in diameter with a
   tracing pencil. The embroidered flowers are scattered around this circle in a border that is approximately 3cm (1$^1/_2$ in) in thickness.
3. Make a bow. Cut a single length of gold wool, tie
   a flat bow and pin it on to your work, placing it
   either at the bottom (as in the picture) or at the
   top. Tack the bow in place with matching cotton
   thread. Fill the shape of the bow with satin stitch
   in a single thread of gold yarn. To make the centre
   of the bow stand out, embroider this section twice.

This will raise the design to make it look like a knot, and higher than the rest of the bow.

4. Using blue yarn, embroider straight stitch as a daisy and scatter the flowers at random around the circle. Embroider small pink rosette stitches at random around the circle.

5. Using bullion rose stitch and deep pink yarn, embroider roses at random around the circle.

6. Put single French knots in the centre of each straight stitch flower, using yellow yarn.

7. Add leaves, using straight stitch in green yarn, embroidering two or three around each flower.

8. Look at the overall shape of your garland and start using stem stitch and French knots to connect the garland, weaving the stems around the flowers.

9. Fill in any spaces in your garland with additional flowers, sewing them in various colours to give a bright effect. Add leaves and stems at random.

10. If the calico looks crumpled, you may press the fabric surrounding the embroidery, but never iron an embroidery as this flattens the stitches.

11. Make up the pillow with a very full deep frill.

A close-up of the stitches used in the Garland Pillow.

POSY WITH BOW PILLOW

MATERIALS

2m (2$^1/_4$yds) calico (this amount allows for a
 full frill and the back of the cushion)
Chenille needle, size 20
Paternayan Persian yarns, colours as follows:

blue 341	purple 311
pink 352	strawberry red 902
yellow 710	green 610
deep pink 351	gold 751

*A close-up of the Posy with Bow Pillow—another
variation on the calico theme.*

INSTRUCTIONS

All the stitches used in this design are illustrated in
Stitch Glossary I.

1. Cut a square of calico 36cm (14in) in diameter.
 Make a bow. (This is the same method as for the
 Garland Pillow. The bow technique is important
 to learn as it is used in many different projects. The
 more bows you make, the better they will look. It
 takes practice to achieve the really even satin
 stitching that gives the finished piece a professional look.) Cut a single length of strawberry red
 wool, tie a flat bow and pin it on to your work.
 Check the photograph for the correct position.
 Tack the bow in place with matching cotton
 thread. Fill the shape of the bow with strawberry
 red satin stitch using a single thread. To make the
 centre of the bow stand out, embroider this section twice.

2. Following the design in the photograph, embroider a posy of flowers using all the stitches illustrated in Stitch Glossary I. Start with daisies, then rosettes and bullion roses. Add French knots to the centre of the flowers, leaves and stems, embroidering the stems to attach to the flowers and lead up through the posy to other flowers. Make sure the posy is balanced and fill in any gaps with additional flowers or leaves.

3. Make up the pillow with a very full deep frill.

CALICO HEART PILLOW

Simple stitches in a heart-shaped garland.

INSTRUCTIONS

1. Cut a square of calico 36cm (14in) in diameter. Trace a heart shape on the centre of the fabric using the template on page 117.
2. Using the same method as for the Garland Pillow on page 19, embroider flowers around the heart shape, following colours and stitches as shown in the close-up photograph and using Stitch Glossary I.
3. Make up the pillow in a heart shape with a very full frill.

LOVE PICTURE

This charming embroidered picture would make a perfect engagement or wedding gift, or to celebrate an anniversary. Select a frame that matches the style of your house—perhaps a birdseye maple timber frame if you want a country effect, or a gilt frame for a more sophisticated look.

MATERIALS

piece of calico 36cm x 38cm (14in x 15in)
DMC cotton yarns:
    white—blanc neige
    pale green 368
white double sided satin ribbon, 2cm (1in) wide
green (to match DMC cotton 368) double sided satin ribbon, 2cm (1in) wide

For the romantic-at-heart, this Love Picture could also be made as a pillow.

INSTRUCTIONS

1. Draw an oval 17cm x 13cm (6$^3/_4$in x 5in) using the template on page 116.
2. Using the alphabet on page 118, trace the letters L O V E inside the oval shape so that they flow together as shown in the diagram. If you make a mistake, erase and try again. It is vital to have the letters positioned correctly before you start stitching.
3. Embroider the letters in the pale green cotton yarn using satin stitch. It is important to make the stitching even—don't rush!

4. Embroider a narrow satin stitch border around the oval outline in the pale green yarn.
5. Make 5 small ribbon roses in white ribbon, using Stitch Glossary II as your guide.
6. Place the white roses on the design, following the diagram, and attach with cotton thread.
7. Tie a bow with green ribbon and attach it to the bottom of the oval.
8. Make 5 green ribbon leaves and place these next to the roses, as shown in the diagram. Embroider French knots above the roses at the top and bottom of the oval.
9. Take your completed work to a framer who understands tapestry stretching. Your embroidery must be stretched properly before it is framed.

POT POURRI BAGS

The pretty pot pourri bags pictured on page 29 were made from small scraps of ribbon, lace and muslin. They can be made from any scraps in your scrap bag. Even a printed fabric can be used, as long as it has a delicate pattern and is complementary to the embroidery. These useful gifts can be made in a few hours.

POT POURRI BAG WITH BLUE BOW

MATERIALS

2 pieces textured lacy white fabric
   8cm x 15cm (3in x 6in)
a piece of blue ribbon
DMC cotton yarns:
    green
    blue
    pink
    yellow

INSTRUCTIONS

1. Take one piece of oblong lacy white fabric.
2. Mark a spot approximately 5cm ($2^1/_2$in) from the bottom of the oblong, where your posy will be.
3. Embroider 3 small daisies in blue cotton yarn in a triangle shape.

4. Add a single pink bullion rose to the centre of the design.
5. Embroider yellow French knots in the centre of each daisy and then add green leaves and stems, as in the diagram.
6. Hand stitch the side seams of the bag and add the lace trim to the top of the bag.
7. Fill the bag with cotton wool and pot pourri (the cotton wool gives a fuller look to the finished bag).
8. Tie the bag with the blue ribbon.

POT POURRI BAG WITH CREAM BOW

MATERIALS

2 pieces muslin fabric 13cm x 15cm (5in x 6in)
a piece of cream ribbon
bow shape, cut from a piece of lace fabric
heavy cotton lace trim
DMC cotton yarns:
    white
    yellow
    green
    blue
    deep blue
    pink

INSTRUCTIONS

1. Hand stitch the cut-out bow to the lower half of the oblong of muslin with white thread.
2. Within the 'wings' of the bow, centre the embroidery design and stitch 3 pink bullion roses—1 large in the centre and 2 small roses.
3. Stitch blue French knots and green leaves below the bullion roses.
4. Stitch 2 deep blue daisies above the bullion roses, with yellow French knots in the centre.

A selection of delicate designs for Pot Pourri Bags, using scraps of fabric and pastel-coloured silks.

5. Complete the design with 3 small pink buds and green leaves at the top.
6. Hand stitch the side seams and attach the cotton lace trim to the top of the bag.
7. Fill the bag with pot pourri and cotton wool and tie with a cream bow.

Pot Pourri Bag with Pink Bow

Materials

2 oblong pieces muslin 14cm x 19cm (5^1/$_2$in x 7^1/$_2$in)
a piece of cotton lace
a length of pink ribbon
heavy cotton lace trim
2m (2^1/$_4$yds) pink double sided satin ribbon, 5mm (^{1}/$_4$in) wide
1^1/$_2$m (1^3/$_4$yds) deep pink pure silk ribbon, 2mm (^{1}/$_8$in) wide
DMC cotton yarns:
    pale pink
    pale green

Instructions

1. Cut out a bow shape from the cotton lace.
2. Hand stitch the cut-out bow to the lower half of the oblong of muslin with white thread.
3. Make 8 flat pink ribbon roses. (See Stitch Glossary II.)
4. Attach the roses to the muslin, following the diagram, and stitch firmly in place with matching cotton thread.
5. Embroider green stems on to the ribbon roses, using stem stitch.
6. Using the pink silk ribbon as yarn, embroider tiny

rosebuds, looping the ribbon to give the effect of buds.

7. Hand stitch the seams. Add the lace trim to the top of the bag.

8. Fill the bag with pot pourri and cotton wool and tie with a deep pink bow.

This Trio of Small Pillows, heavily trimmed with lace, uses the basic stitches again, but this time with silk instead of wool yarns.

TRIO OF SMALL PILLOWS

These charming pillows are very simple to make. They use the basic techniques we have shown you using wool embroidery, but this time we use silk fabrics and DMC cotton yarns instead of wools. Each pillow can be worked in a very short time and they make ideal gifts.

GARLAND PILLOW WITH RIBBON ROSES AND EMBROIDERY

MATERIALS

1m (1yd, 5in) white silk fabric
DMC cotton yarns:
    white
    lemon
    blue
    pink
    mauve
    green
3m ($3^1/_2$yds) white double sided satin
    ribbon, 5mm ($^1/_4$ in) wide

INSTRUCTIONS

1. Cut an oblong of white silk fabric 25cm x 20cm (10in x 8in).

2. Hem the edges of the fabric in tacking stitch to stop fraying.
3. Draw a circle approximately 14cm (5^1/$_2$in) in diameter.
4. Make 6 ribbon roses in white satin ribbon (see Stitch Glossary II).
5. Place the roses at random around the circle. Secure the roses with white cotton yarn, then pin down the outside petals of each rose with embroidered leaves in green (see straight stitch in Stitch Glossary I).
6. Proceed as with the calico Garland Pillow on page 19, filling the circle with embroidered flowers, using the stitches in Stitch Glossary I.
7. Make up the cushion with a full deep frill.

LACE TRIMMED PILLOW

MATERIALS

$^1/_4$ m (10in) white silk fabric
1m (1yd, 5in) Chantilly lace (for frill)
DMC cotton yarns:
    white
    blue
    pale pink
    pink
    gold
    yellow
3m ($3^1/_2$ yds) white double sided satin
   ribbon, 5mm ($^1/_4$ in) wide

INSTRUCTIONS

1. Cut an oblong of white silk fabric 20cm x 25cm (8in x 10in).
2. Draw a small circle approximately 10cm (4in) in diameter.
3. Embroider around the outline with double chain stitch (see stem stitch in Stitch Glossary I), using 6 strands white cotton yarn.
4. Make 6 ribbon roses (see Stitch Glossary II) in white satin ribbon. Stitch 3 roses at the top and 3 at the bottom of the circle.
5. Add small embroidered rosebuds, French knots and leaves (see Stitch Glossary I) as shown in the diagram.
6. Make up the cushion, using Chantilly lace for the frill.

SMALL SILK CUSHION
WITH FLOWER POSY,
TRIMMED WITH LACE

MATERIALS

$1/_4$m (10in) white silk fabric
1m (1yd, 5in) Chantilly lace (for frill)
DMC cotton yarns:
    purple
    mauve
    cerise
    gold
    yellow

blue
turquoise
green
peach
(These colours are just a guide. You may like
to select shades that blend with your own
colour scheme.)

INSTRUCTIONS

1. Cut a square piece of white silk fabric, approximately 20cm x 20cm (8in x 8in).
2. Following the diagram, embroider the flowers, stems and bow. The technique is similar to that used for the calico Posy with Bow pillow on page 21, but on a smaller scale and using DMC cotton yarns instead of wool. Use 6 strands of cotton threaded through the needle from top to bottom (see General Hints, page 5). For the stems of the posy, use only 2 strands of cotton, or the posy will look too heavy at the base.
3. Make up the cushion, using Chantilly lace for the trim.

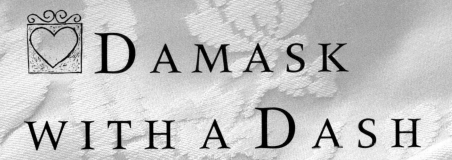

DAMASK WITH A DASH

This charming all-white bedroom uses embroidered pillows and different weights and textures of damask for a serene effect.

D AMASK is a traditional fabric that has been used for centuries, in a variety of weights and designs. The name originates from the beautifully patterned silks woven in Damascus during the 12th Century and taken to Europe by Marco Polo. It is a jacquard fabric that has patterns similar to those in brocade, but with a flatter surface. In damask any combination of two of the three basic weaves may be used for the pattern and the background, provided that the weave of the pattern differs from that of the background. The pattern is made visible by the effect of light striking the different portions of the fabric in the different weaves. The pattern effect is usually reversible. Originally made from silk, damasks are now made of linen, cotton, wool and any of the synthetic fibres, or of combinations of the two.

Traditionally damask has been used for draperies and upholstery, and in more recent times cotton damask was used to bring an air of elegance to the dining table.

In the 1990s damask is enjoying renewed popularity. Several major bed linen manufacturers have introduced ranges in damask and we are seeing a revival of the fabric in an exciting selection of colours, including crimson, blue and lemon.

Damask is available in a variety of weights and, for decorating purposes, it is important to choose the correct weight to suit the task in hand. For example, heavier weights are ideal for upholstery on a dining chair or couch, and lighter weights for bed linen, tablecloths and cushions.

For embroidery, select a damask fabric with a complementary jacquard pattern, making sure that it won't compete with the embroidery.

The white-on-white bedroom illustrated on page 40 is a simple but very effective style which looks good in a town or country setting. For a country mood, a simple decor looks best—a white cotton throwover, white sheets and pillowcases, a mosquito net suspended from a hook in the ceiling, and baskets of fresh flowers. Bedside tables can be covered with floor-length cloths, and an antique trunk at the foot of the bed will provide additional blanket storage. Simple candlestick lamps add atmosphere and white-on-white embroidered pillows (in a variety of shapes and sizes) scattered on the bed are the finishing touch.

For a more sophisticated approach, use a pine green coloured damask for a bedspread, trimmed with a lavish braided fringe. Seek out an interesting bed head—it doesn't have to be a costly antique—a reproduction bed head, stripped and waxed, can have just the same effect as a genuine antique piece. Add a gilt mirror, some ornate accessories such as silver or gold photo frames, classic bedside lights, and when the budget allows, a handsome armoire. A fake fur throwover at the end of the bed is the ultimate touch of luxury.

When decorating with damask in deep shades, embroidered silks and taffetas in rich colours will complement the damask wonderfully. Try embroidered silk pillows with fringes in jewel colours on the dark green damask.

Pair of Initialled Damask Pillows

Initialled Damask Pillow

Materials

2m (2^1/$_4$yds) white damask
DMC cotton thread:
    white—blanc neige
    green 503
white double sided satin ribbon, 5mm
    (^{1}/$_4$in) wide

Instructions

1. Cut out a square of damask 41cm x 41cm (16in x 16in).
2. Draw an oval in the centre of the damask square using the template on page 116.
3. Trace your chosen initial in the centre of the oval using the alphabet on page 118.
4. Stitch the initial in satin stitch in white cotton thread.
5. Double chain stitch (see stem stitch in Stitch Glossary I) around the oval using the green cotton thread.
6. Make 9 white ribbon roses (see Stitch Glossary II).
7. Place 5 roses in the centre at the top of the oval (see diagram). Place 4 roses in the centre at the bottom of the oval. Pin all the roses in place and stitch them down using the white cotton thread.
8. Embroider leaves using straight stitch (see Stitch

Glossary I), scattering them around the roses at the top and bottom of the design (see diagram).

9. At the bottom of the design, embroider clusters of French knots in white, shaping them down to a point at the base of the design. Connect each knot in flat stitch with a single green thread, linking them to look as if they are growing from a single stem.

10. Then add white French knots to the top of the oval (see diagram). Connect each knot with a single green thread to look as though they are growing.

11. Make up the pillow with a full wide frill.

The most personal of gifts—an initialled pillow.

INITIALLED CREST PILLOW

MATERIALS

2m (2¹/₄yds) white or cream damask
DMC cotton thread:
    green 504
    pink 819
    blue/grey 932
    ecru
    white

INSTRUCTIONS

1. Cut a square pillow shape 38cm x 38cm (15in x 15in). Trace a small oval shape on the fabric 5cm x 4 cm (2¹/₂in x 2in).

2. Draw your selected initial on the centre of the oval.

3. Embroider the initial in satin stitch with white cotton thread if using white damask as a base cloth, or with ecru if using cream damask.

4. Make 5 ribbon roses in cream silk ribbon (see Stitch Glossary III) and 8 ribbon roses using pink silk ribbon.

5. Place the roses on the design, following the shape in the diagram: 2 cream roses at the top of the oval, 6 pink roses placed at intervals around the oval, 1 cream rose in the centre at the base of the oval and 2 cream roses on either side of the top of the oval.

6. Embroider bullion roses (see Stitch Glossary I) in blue/grey cotton thread on either side of the top and bottom cream silk ribbon roses. Embroider bullion roses in pink cotton thread on either side of the pink silk ribbon roses.

7. Using silk ribbon threaded through the needle to be used as yarn, embroider three flowers in straight stitch as a daisy (see Stitch Glossary II), one at the base of the design, and on the right and left of the 'wings' of the design.

8. Add French knots in white or ecru cotton thread below each of the embroidered silk ribbon roses, and above the twin roses at the top of the design.

A pastel embroidered crest on a white damask pillow, trimmed with green and pink satin ribbons.

Detail of the pastel embroidered crest.

9. Using straight stitch, add leaves and stems to the French knots, and to trim each rose (see diagram), making sure that the design matches and balances.

10. Make up the cushion with a full deep frill, and inserts of narrow pink and green ribbons.

TABLECLOTH AND NAPKINS

This elegant table setting illustrates damask at its very best. The look is luxurious but the embroidery is simple—and the finished result, a beautiful heirloom tablecloth and napkins to be handed down through the family.

Choose any colour damask to blend with your particular style—the gold embroidery would look good on any colour fabric, or instead of using gold thread, a tone-on-tone design (for example, cream embroidery on cream damask, or white embroidery on white damask) is very chic.

MATERIALS

Measure your dining table and buy sufficient
   damask fabric for the table size, allowing for
   a drop at the sides of the table.
Allow $1/2$m (20in) damask per napkin,
   depending on the width of the fabric.
gold lurex embroidery thread
gold lurex edging braid

NAPKINS

INSTRUCTIONS

1. Cut out the napkins, 50cm x 50cm (20in x 20in).
   Draw the initial on to one corner of each napkin.
2. Following the diagram and using gold thread,

Close-up of a gold embroidered initial design on the napkin and tablecloth.

embroider the initial in satin stitch and small bullion roses. Link the flowers with tiny stem stitch.

3. Following the diagram, draw a curved spray of flowers beneath the initial. Embroider with gold thread, linking the bullion roses with stem stitch and leaf stitch.

4. Hem the napkins, incorporating the gold braid edging. Use bias binding on the back of the napkin for a neat finish.

TABLECLOTH

INSTRUCTIONS

1. Cut the damask to tablecloth size.

2. In each corner of the cloth, draw a circle approximately 7cm (2³/₄in) in diameter.

3. In the centre of each circle trace the initial. Using gold thread, embroider the initial in satin stitch and tiny bullion roses, as for the napkin.

4. Following the diagram, embroider a garland around the circle using tiny bullion roses, and leaf, straight and stem stitches.

5. Make a small flowing bow at one side of the garland and embroider it in satin stitch, following the technique used in the Garland Pillow on page 19.

6. Make up the tablecloth, incorporating the gold braid edging.

7. Use with pride!

An heirloom tablecloth and napkins, luxuriously embroidered with gold thread, sets the scene for a celebration.

SATINS AND SILKS

The corner of this sitting room has a selection of richly embroidered satin and silk cushions on a plain couch.

THE 'faded country house' look will always be popular—a comfortable low-key approach to decorating that is ideal for family life. But if you are thinking of revamping your house this year, a more luxurious approach is worth considering. This does not have to mean thousands of dollars—it is the look of luxury you are after, without necessarily having a luxurious income to match!

Today's designers love texture; velvet with satin, taffeta with tartan, ruching, fringes, and a general air of opulence. It is the volume of fabric that gives the look of luxury. Austrian blinds, an opulent look, take a lot of fabric but by using dress taffeta, you can achieve the right look for a low outlay. Decorating stores also sell ready-made Austrian blinds. For the ultimate in simple window treatments, wind a length of fabric around a curtain pole, looping at each end, to drop to the floor. Tie the drop lengths with big bows and you have instant glamour.

Always keep your eyes open for furniture bargains. Bedroom chairs, for instance, are often overlooked and can be a bargain buy. Because they are small the dealers think they are not useful, but an extra chair often comes in handy in the sitting room, a child's room or in an apartment. A small chair will not require metres of fabric to cover it, so a remnant of fabric will do the job. The green moiré chair on page 68 was bought for $50 at a street market. Now reupholstered in sea green moiré taffeta with embroidered cushions to match, the chair has loads of style and is extremely comfortable too.

GILT-EDGED POSY PICTURE

This is the design for the embroiderer who wants the maximum effect for the minimum effort! Using extravagant jacquard fabric from Valentino, (we used a remnant) a tiny posy of multi-coloured ribbon roses has been framed in an opulent gilt frame—an almost decadent approach to embroidered decoration.

MATERIALS

25cm (10in) Valentino or other luxurious fabric
satin ribbons, 5mm ($^1/_4$ in) wide in the
    following colours:
        purple—2 shades
        orange
        hot pink
        cerise
        mustard yellow
        sage green
DMC cotton thread:
        cerise pink
        pink
        gold
        forest green
        purple 1.
        purple 2.

INSTRUCTIONS

1. If using a jacquard fabric, make sure you centre the posy on the jacquard design.

2. Make ribbon rosebuds as follows: 2 hot pink, 2 cerise, 4 orange, 2 in each shade of purple and 4 mustard.

3. Place the roses on the fabric in a posy shape and pin in position. You may want to arrange and re-arrange this several times until you are happy with the shape and colour balance. Sew the ribbon rosebuds onto the fabric using matching cotton thread.

4. Embroider daisies (see Stitch Glossary I) in cerise pink and purple, filling in the gaps between the ribbon roses.

5. Add gold French knots to the centre of the daisies.

6. Using sage green ribbon as yarn (see Stitch Glossary III), stitch 'stems' onto the posy, overlapping them to look like real flowers. Make sure that you stitch these very loosely.

7. Tie a small bow in purple ribbon around the stems of the posy and fasten it with cotton thread.

8. Take the finished work to a framer, making sure the embroidery is stretched before framing. Also ensure the framer understands that you require the embroidery to be recessed in the frame.

This tiny posy of ribbon roses achieves its effect through the blending of rich colours on a sumptuous fabric.

CREAM AND WHITE PILLOW WITH RIBBON ROSES AND BOW

MATERIALS

$^1/_2$m (20in) white cotton fabric
3m (3$^1/_2$yds) broderie anglaise (for frill)
DMC cotton thread:
    white 712
    pale green 504
5m (11yds) cream double sided silk ribbon,
    5mm ($^1/_4$in) wide

INSTRUCTIONS

Throughout this project, use 2 strands of cotton thread in the needle for the embroidery.

1. Make a bow design using white cotton thread.
2. Satin stitch the bow shape in white thread.
3. Make 32 cream silk ribbon roses. It doesn't matter if they aren't all exactly the same size.
4. Pin the ribbon roses on to the cotton fabric, making a posy shape. The proportion is important—balance the roses to suit the bow. You may need to rearrange the roses several times. Don't hurry! Pin the roses on—leave the work and see how it looks the next day. If you're not happy with it, do it again in a different arrangement. Stitch the roses on to the fabric with white cotton thread, making sure that the stitches are invisible.
5. Embroider white French knots at the base of each rose, to resemble gypsophila (see diagram). Add

stem stitch in green cotton thread to connect each ribbon rose, and leaf stitch in green on the edges of the outside roses.

6. Make up the pillow using the broderie anglaise for deep wide double frills.

An elegant bedroom accessory—this Cream and White Pillow with Ribbon Roses and Bow.

FRAMED PASTEL BOUQUET

Yet another variation on the pastel theme, this picture incorporates silk ribbon rosebuds and embroidered flowers in a pastel bouquet.

MATERIALS

$^1/_2$m (20in) pure silk fabric
DMC cotton thread:

blue 1.	apricot 2.
blue 2.	pale pink
mauve 1.	green 1.
mauve 2.	green 2.
lemon 1.	green 3.
lemon 2.	brown 1.
apricot 1.	brown 2.

1m ($1^1/_4$yds) each pure silk ribbons, 2.5mm ($^1/_8$in) wide:

pink	cream
lemon	mid-green
mauve	pale green
burgundy	

double sided satin ribbon, 5mm ($^1/_4$in) wide:
cream—1m ($1^1/_4$yds)
dusty pink—$^1/_4$m (10in)

Silk ribbon rosebuds and embroidered flowers combined in an old-fashioned bouquet.

INSTRUCTIONS

1. Make ribbon roses in colours according to the photograph or colours to suit your house.
2. Following the diagram, place the roses on to the fabric and stitch in place.

3. Embroider rosettes, using silk ribbon as yarn (see Stitch Glossary I).
4. Embroider rosettes using the coloured cotton thread, following the diagram.
5. Fill in around the posy with embroidered flowers and leaves in cotton thread.
6. Embroider stems in stem stitch (see Stitch Glossary I), some using 2 strands cotton thread, others using 4 strands, to give varied texture.
7. Wrap the stems in dusty pink ribbon, fastening in the front.
8. Take the finished piece to the framer, making sure that the embroidery is stretched before mounting. A double mount is recommended—the darker mount immediately edging the embroidery, the paler mount highlighting the shades of the work.

NIGHTGOWN AND ROBE

Forget about wash and wear—this is all about luxury and glamour! We've taken a classic satin robe and nightgown and embroidered them with simple designs, adding that individual touch of panache. Buy any classic sleepwear (or make your own) and embroider a complementary design that lifts the lingerie out of the ordinary.

The lingerie bag and padded hanger (see Perfect Presents for instructions for the hanger) are glamorous accessories for your own wardrobe or would make elegant gifts. The slippers were made especially for the photograph.

MATERIALS

Be sure to match the ribbon and silk shades to
  your chosen garments.
1 satin nightgown
1 tailored satin gown
$2^1/_2$m ($2^3/_4$yds) double sided satin ribbon,
  5mm ($^1/_4$in) wide
2m ($2^1/_4$yds) silk embroidery ribbon, 2.5mm
  ($^1/_8$in) wide
DMC cotton thread:
  green
  apricot 1.
  apricot 2.
  (or matched to the shade of the gown)

INSTRUCTIONS

The designs used on both the nightgown and the robe are similar—shaped in a horseshoe around the centre of the nightgown yoke and on the pocket of the robe.

NIGHTGOWN

1. Make 3 ribbon roses (see Stitch Glossary II) from the double sided satin ribbon.
2. Place the ribbon roses in the centre of the yoke, as illustrated in the photograph.
3. Add embroidered rosebuds using bullion rose stitch, (see Stitch Glossary I) following the diagram.
4. Complete the design with ribbon rosebuds (see Stitch Glossary II) and embroidered leaves and stems.

ROBE

Follow instructions for nightgown, embroidering design on robe pocket. Add embroidered bullion rose with leaves to the corners of the collar.

Close-up detail of nightgown yoke embroidery.

Close-up detail of dressing gown pocket embroidery.

A classic satin robe and nightgown embroidered in matching silks.

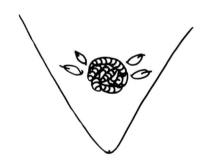

LINGERIE BAG

MATERIALS

1m (1¹/₄yds) apricot moiré taffeta
4m (4¹/₄yds) double sided satin ribbon, 5mm
   (¹/₄ in) wide
2m (2¹/₄yds) silk embroidery ribbon, 2.5mm
   (¹/₈in) wide
DMC cotton thread:
   apricot
   green

INSTRUCTIONS

1. Cut a piece of apricot moiré taffeta 43cm x 48cm (17 x 19in).
2. Trace a heart shape on the centre of the fabric using the template on page 117.
3. Make a bow, placing the centre above the heart shape (see diagram) and embroider using the technique desribed in Posy with Bow Pillow on page 21.
4. Fill in the bow using satin stitch.
5. Make 12 ribbon roses, varying in size, using double sided satin ribbon. (See Stitch Glossary II.)
6. Place the roses on the heart, as shown in the diagram, and stitch in place.

7. Complete the heart with embroidered bullion roses, silk ribbon rosebuds, (see Stitch Glossary II) leaves and stems.
8. Make up the lingerie bag with a drawstring top.

An embroidered lingerie bag—a delightful gift for a special occasion.
(The slippers were commissioned to match the nightgown and robe.)

RUCHED GREEN MOIRÉ PILLOW WITH RIBBON EMBROIDERY

This pillow uses all the basic stitchery shown in Stitch Glossary I but employs ribbon instead of wool or cotton yarns for the main design features. Cotton yarns are used as fill-in stitches. It is very simple to do.

MATERIALS

$1^{1}/_{2}$m ($1^{3}/_{4}$yds) green moiré taffeta
5m ($5^{3}/_{4}$yds) pink pure silk ribbon, 5mm ($^{1}/_{4}$ in) wide
2m ($2^{1}/_{4}$yds) green pure silk ribbon, 2.5mm ($^{1}/_{8}$mm) wide
DMC cotton yarns:
    pink
    green
    pale pink
    gold

INSTRUCTIONS

1. Trace 2 half circles from the diagram in the centre of a 38cm (15in) square piece of moiré taffeta.
2. Using pink silk ribbon as yarn, embroider flowers in straight stitch, 2 at the top of the design and 2 at the base. Use short pieces of ribbon to avoid twisting and make sure the stitches (petals) are uneven in length (see diagram).
3. Add half flowers in pink ribbon either side of the large flowers.

4. Embroider satin stitch decoration at top and bottom and on either side of the design in pink cotton thread, following the diagram.

5. Using straight stitch with green ribbon as yarn, embroider large leaves, as shown in the diagram. Link up the pink ribbon flowers with satin stitch in green cotton thread.

6. Add French knots in pink cotton thread, as shown in the diagram, and link the flowers with straight stitch in green cotton thread.

7. Make up the cushion using a ruched edging in green moiré taffeta, with pale pink moiré piping to match the shade of the pink ribbon flowers.

This green moiré pillow is very simple to embroider—the use of colour and texture gives a high-fashion look.

ADVANCED STITCHERY

FIVE PILLOWS

These cushions are shown in the photograph on page 72. The design and colour theme of these cushions were taken from the opulent tasselled fringes. They employ advanced yarn and ribbon embroidery techniques. We illustrate a colour scheme as an example, but suggest you develop your own, depending on the fringe colour you select to match your decor.

CLARET MOIRÉ TAFFETA TASSELLED PILLOW

MATERIALS

$^1/_2$m (20in) claret moiré taffeta
1m (1$^1/_4$yds) fringe
1 card claret silk ribbon, 2.5mm ($^1/_8$in) wide
$^1/_2$ m (20in) gold double sided ribbon, 5mm ($^1/_4$in) wide
DMC cotton thread:
    dark green
    gold

INSTRUCTIONS

1. Tie a bow with a piece of the gold cotton thread and place in the centre of a 30cm (12in) square piece of claret moiré taffeta, using the same method

(Previous spread) Maximum decorating impact has been achieved here. On this sofa five taffeta cushions have been embroidered in different ways, using the same colour palette and fringing, tassles and braid.

as described on page 19 for the calico Garland Pillow.

2. Satin stitch the bow in gold cotton thread, making sure that the stitches are very even and loose.

3. Make 10 gold silk ribbon roses (see Stitch Glossary II) in double sided ribbon, varying in size.

4. Place the roses on the cushion and stitch in place, following the diagram.

5. Using satin ribbon as yarn, embroider 13 rosettes as shown in the diagram. (See Stitch Glossary I.)

6. Embroider the rosebuds using silk ribbon as yarn, making sure they flow with the design. (See Stitch Glossary I: small bud flowers.)

7. Connect all rosebuds with green cotton thread in stem stitch.

8. Add leaves here and there (see diagram), in green cotton thread.

9. Make up with fringe edging. Add tassels to each corner for that over-the-top opulence!

The design theme for this pillow started with the French braid trim which was teamed with ribbon flowers and silk embroidery on claret moiré taffeta. (Instructions on page 74.)

GOLD MOIRÉ CUSHION WITH CORDED EDGE AND ALL RIBBON EMBROIDERY

Using two types of ribbon for the roses, this cushion is a good example of ribbon embroidery techniques.

MATERIALS

$1^1/_2$m ($1^3/_4$yds) gold moiré taffeta
2m ($2^1/_4$yds) gold cord trim
2m ($2^1/_4$yds) yellow pure silk ribbon, 2.5mm ($^1/_8$in) wide
double sided ribbon, 5mm ($^1/_4$in) wide:
    pink $1^1/_2$m ($1^3/_4$yds)
    blue $1^1/_2$m ($1^3/_4$yds)
    deep gold $1^1/_2$m ($1^3/_4$yds)
    yellow 3m ($3^1/_2$yds)
$2^1/_2$m ($2^3/_4$yds) shaded green ribbon

A gold moiré taffeta cushion with pastel ribbon embroidery, finished with braid and a ruched edge.

INSTRUCTIONS

1. Make 7 ribbon roses in yellow pure silk ribbon. (See Stitch Glossary II.)
2. Make 8 rosebuds in yellow pure silk ribbon.
3. Make 8 ribbon roses in double sided ribbon, 5mm ($^1/_4$in) wide, following the colours in the diagram, 3 pink, 3 blue and 2 gold.
4. Make 15 leaves in shaded green ribbon. (See Stitch Glossary II.)
5. Place the leaves on the design according to the diagram, balancing the design on the watermarked moiré, and stitch down with cotton thread, making sure that the stitches do not show.
6. Place the roses on the fabric, following the diagram, and stitch down.
7. Add rosebuds around the edge of the design.
8. Using pure silk ribbon as yarn, embroider rosebuds, following the diagram for placement. (See Stitch Glossary I.)

9. Link all the flowers with stem stitch in green cotton thread.
10. Make up the cushion, using ruched edging. The gold cord trim is optional.

RED MOIRÉ CUSHION WITH VELVET APPLIQUÉ

This exotic small pillow was made from scraps of material in the work basket. This type of design can use silk or velvet remnants and cord.

MATERIALS

$^1/_2$m (20in) burgundy moiré taffeta
$^3/_4$m (29in) burgundy crushed velvet ribbon, 4cm (2in) wide
$^1/_2$m (20in) burgundy crushed velvet ribbon, 2cm (1in) wide
5m ($5^3/_4$yds) pure silk embroidery ribbon, 2.5mm ($^1/_8$in) wide
2m ($2^1/_4$yds) gold cord
a small piece of cream linen
DMC cotton thread:
    dark green
    burgundy

INSTRUCTIONS

1. Take the small piece of cream linen, approximately 13cm x 10cm (5in x 4in) and trace the initial in the centre, using the alphabet on page 118.
2. Embroider the initial in satin stitch, using the burgundy cotton thread.
3. Cut an oblong of burgundy moiré taffeta, 28cm x 38cm (11in x 15in).
4. Baste the embroidered piece of linen on to the centre of the rectangle of taffeta, stitching firmly around the edge.
5. Take the 2cm (1in) wide burgundy velvet ribbon and place it as a frame around the edges of the linen. Stitch it in place securely.
6. Stitch gold cord around the outside of the crushed velvet 'frame'.
7. Following the diagram, embroider rosettes and

rosebuds using the burgundy pure silk ribbon as yarn (see Stitch Glossary III). Add stems and leaves in the green cotton thread.

8. Make up the cushion using the crushed velvet ribbon, 4cm (2in) wide, as a border on each end, as shown in the photograph, and outline the borders with gold cord.

Rich red scraps from the work basket have been given a new life in this glamourous initialled pillow.

The French braid was the starting point for this heart-shaped pillow, embroidered with a simple garland design.

HEART SHAPED MOIRÉ CUSHION

MATERIALS

$^1/_2$m (20in) yellow moiré taffeta

1m (1yd, 5in) decorative fringe, in colours to
   blend with the moiré taffeta

4m (4$^1/_2$yds) yellow double sided ribbon, 5mm
   ($^1/_4$in) wide

1$^1/_2$m (1$^3/_4$yds) yellow pure silk ribbon,
   2.5mm ($^1/_8$in) wide

DMC cotton thread:
   green
   pink 1.
   pink 2.
   pink 3.

INSTRUCTIONS

1. Cut a 33cm (13in) square of yellow moiré taffeta.

2. Using the template on page 117, draw an oval on
   the fabric, making sure that the watermark is
   centred. Embroider the outline of the oval in stem
   stitch (see Stitch Glossary I) using yellow cotton
   thread in 6 strands. Using pale pink cotton thread,
   'wrap' around the stem outline (see diagram).

3. Using double sided ribbon, make 6 yellow ribbon
   roses. Place on the design as shown in the diagram
   and stitch.

4. Using yellow ribbon as yarn, embroider 4 daisies
   (see Stitch Glossary I).

5. Add yellow rosebuds made from the pure silk
   ribbon at the top and bottom and on both sides of
   the design.

6. Using two shades of pink cotton thread, scatter
   embroidered buds in flat stitch. Using the palest
   pink thread, scatter French knots to match the
   diagram.

7. Add yellow French knots in the cotton thread at

the top and base of the design. Embroider the stems in pale green cotton thread.

8. Make up into a heart shaped cushion, trimming the edge with decorative fringe. Add a tassel at the base of the heart.

GOLD MOIRÉ PILLOW WITH ORNATE FRINGE AND PADDED EMBROIDERY

This stunning pillow looks difficult to make, but in fact still only uses the basic stitches in Stitch Glossary I. The design is very closely packed, using tiny stitches, and requires patience to execute. The embroidery is done on calico fabric which is then cut out and remounted with padding on to the moiré taffeta. The lavish braid was the inspiration for the design and the colour scheme suggested itself. To make a similar cushion, the colours you use will depend entirely on the colours in the braid.

Always buy the fringe first—then develop your colour scheme second, not the other way around!

MATERIALS

$^1/_2$m (20in) gold moiré taffeta
$^1/_4$m (10in) calico
$1^1/_4$m ($1^1/_2$yds) French fringe
DMC cotton thread:

burgundy	green 2.
gold	green 3.
orange	yellow
blue 1.	pink
blue 2.	terracotta
cream	lilac
green 1.	scarlet

INSTRUCTIONS

1. Cut a square of calico 31cm x 31cm (12in x 12in).
2. Draw a circle 13cm (5in) in diameter.
3. Make 4 small bows in the centre of each side of the circle (see diagram). For the method, see the Garland Pillow on page 19. Embroider the bows in satin stitch using the burgundy thread.
4. Embroider a garland design using all the stitches

in Stitch Glossary I, in coloured thread to match the fringe. Pack the flowers tightly, using small stitches, and balance the circle.

5. Cut out the embroidery with fine scissors, leaving a 5mm ($^1/_4$in) hem both inside and outside the circle of flowers.

6. Cut a square of moiré taffeta 28cm (11in). Pin the garland to the centre of the square, tacking the inside of the garland first, turning in the hem of the calico. Use cotton wool for the padding and gradually tack down the outside of the garland, turning in the calico hem and padding the design

This pillow illustrates a new technique—padded embroidery. The garland was embroidered on calico, cut out and mounted on the moiré fabric.

as you go. Make sure that the padding is even on all sides.

7. Finally, disguise the inside and outside edges of the attached embroidery with decorative stitches such as French knots, tiny flowers and leaves. Overstitch the bows for additional emphasis.

8. Make up the cushion, with the French fringe on the border.

GREEN MOIRÉ STOOL

This attractive design is simple to stitch, using all the basic embroidery stitches in Stitch Glossary I. Its charm lies in the subtle shading of the colours used in the design. Each flower is embroidered in two different shades of pink.

MATERIALS

$^3/_4$m (30in) pale green moiré taffeta
  (to match DMC cotton thread 502)
DMC cotton thread:
    green 502
    green 504
    pink 3354
    pink 818
    pink 778
    pink 442
1 stool

INSTRUCTIONS

1. Before starting this project, check the position of the watermark on the moiré taffeta and centre the design so that the embroidery is even on both sides. Place the piece of taffeta over the stool and tie a large bow in cotton thread, in a central position on the fabric, using the same method outlined in the Garland Pillow on page 19. Spread the ribbon shape along the sides and towards the top of the design, as shown in the diagram.

2. When you are happy with the shape of the bow, tack it down with thread and embroider in satin stitch over the tacked cotton to resemble a flowing ribbon. Do not embroider tightly—loose stitches are crucial to this design.

3. Complete the design by following the diagram, using stitches as illustrated and colours as shown in the photograph.

4. Take the completed work to a reputable upholsterer and have the embroidery upholstered onto the stool, with rouleau piping in moiré taffeta around the circumference.

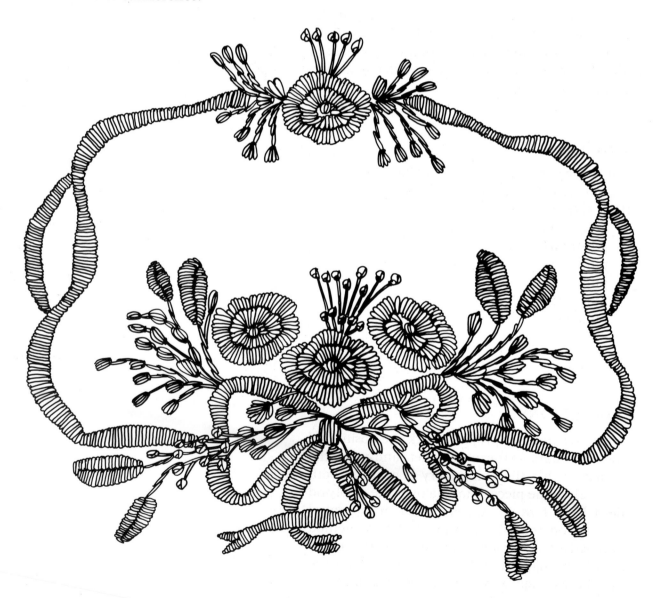

This embroidered stool was designed to coordinate with the bedroom chair on page 68.

Close-up of the flowing design on the green moiré stool.

CREAM FRINGED FOOTSTOOL

French fringing was the inspiration for this footstool.
The remnant was found in a fabric showroon and the
embroidery was designed to complement the beautiful delicate colours in the fringe. Any fringe could
be used in a similar way, building the colour theme
around the shades of the fringe.

MATERIALS

$^1/_2$m (20in) cream slubbed silk fabric
French fringe
$1^1/_2$m ($1^3/_4$yds) pink double sided satin ribbon,
 5mm ($^1/_4$in) wide
3m ($3^1/_2$yds) blue double sided satin ribbon,
 5mm ($^1/_4$in) wide
2m ($2^1/_4$yds) cream double sided satin ribbon,
 5mm ($^1/_4$in) wide
$1^1/_2$m ($1^3/_4$yds) pink pure silk embroidery
 ribbon, 2.5mm ($^1/_8$in) wide
2m ($2^1/_4$yds) blue pure silk embroidery ribbon,
 2.5mm ($^1/_8$in) wide
$1^1/_2$m ($1^3/_4$yds) cream pure silk embroidery
 ribbon, 2.5mm ($^1/_8$in) wide
DMC cotton thread to match the ribbons:
 pink
 blue
 cream

INSTRUCTIONS

1. Cut a 38cm (15in) square of the cream slubbed silk fabric.

2. Draw a rectangle on to the fabric, 15cm x 19cm (6in x $7\frac{1}{2}$in), in the centre of the square of silk fabric.

3. Make ribbon roses, using the double sided satin ribbon, as follows: 10 blue, 6 cream and 3 pink.

4. Following the diagram, place the ribbon roses on the fabric and attach them with the cream thread.

5. Embroider rosettes, using silk ribbon as yarn, following the diagram. (See Stitch Glossary I.) Use your own discretion about the colours, to blend with the satin ribbon roses.

6. Embroider flowerbuds and French knots in the DMC cotton thread, as shown in the diagram. Put them around each ribbon rose cluster, in the corners of the rectangle, and halfway between each corner. (Sew pink buds next to pink ribbon roses, cream buds next to cream ribbon roses, etc.)

7. Stitch flowerbuds around the ribbon roses in the middle of the design.

8. Using stem stitch, embroider stems in green cotton thread, and add leaves where required.

9. Outline the border of the rectangle with double chain stitch in cream cotton thread. Twist blue pure silk ribbon around each chain stitch, giving a wrapped effect.

10. Take the stool and the embroidery to an upholsterer and have the embroidery upholstered on to the stool, with the French fringe border.

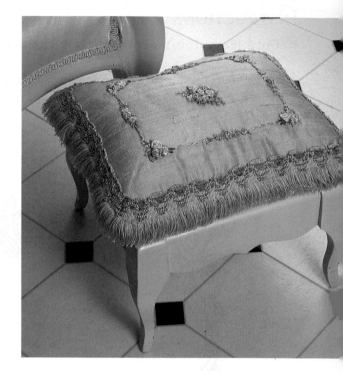

A cream footstool made from a fabric remnant, stitched in pastel colours and edged with French braid.

SUMMER GARDEN PICTURE

This embroidered picture has a nostalgic mood reminiscent of the 1920s. Sewn on moiré taffeta, with a matching mount, the 'Summer Garden' flowers are worked in the palette of a herbaceous border.

This summer garden picture has a matching moiré taffeta mount. (It is important to match the water marks.)

MATERIALS

$\frac{1}{2}$m (20in) cream moiré taffeta
1m ($1\frac{1}{4}$yds) white satin ribbon, 5mm
    ($\frac{1}{4}$in) wide
DMC cotton thread:
    white
    yellow
    pink
    green
    lilac

INSTRUCTIONS

1. Cut a piece of cream moiré taffeta, 31cm x33cm (12in x 13in).
2. Make 2 ribbon roses with the white satin ribbon and place them in the centre of the fabric. Attach them with white thread.
3. Following the diagram, embroider flowers and leaves in a tightly packed design, but stitch loosely! The centre flowers are all over stitched, giving a padded effect, but outside stitches are embroidered just once in the normal way.

4. Take the completed work to a framer who understands the importance of stretching the embroidery. The mount around the embroidery is made
   from the same cream moiré taffeta and the water-
   marks must be matched. Choose a simple frame to
   accentuate the delicacy of the stitching.

LESLIE'S ROSE DREAM

This pillow demonstrates a new technique combining two different fabrics, velvet and damask, embroidered with overblown peony roses, and trimmed with gold cord. This romantic look can be translated into many different effects, using whatever fabrics you happen to have on hand. This is the ideal cushion to make from the remnants of expensive fabrics you occasionally find on sale in decorator stores. The colour shading in the peony roses is also a new technique.

MATERIALS

1m (1yd, 5in) pale green jacquard damask
23cm (9in) square of dark green velvet
1m ($1^1/_4$yds) thick gold cord
$^1/_2$m (20in) fine gold cord
$1^1/_2$m ($1^3/_4$yds) deep pink double sided satin
    ribbon, 1cm ($^1/_2$in) wide
1m ($1^1/_4$yds) medium pink double sided satin
    ribbon, 20mm ($^3/_4$in) wide
1m ($1^1/_4$yds) pale pink double sided satin
    ribbon, 2cm (1in) wide
1m ($1^1/_4$yds) gold rayon ribbon
1m ($1^1/_4$yds) green rayon ribbon
DMC cotton thread:
    pink

INSTRUCTIONS

1. Cut a 23cm (9in) square of the green velvet fabric.
2. Make 2 large full-blown peony roses, and one smaller peony rose, following the instructions in Stitch Glossary II, but shading the flowers and using different widths of ribbon, as above. Keep building up the flowers until you have the desired fullness.
3. Following the diagram, attach the roses to the green velvet, making sure that they are very secure, and without showing the stitches used to attach them.
4. Add one small rosebud, as in the diagram.
5. Using the gold rayon ribbon as thread, embroider leaves, following the diagram.
6. Using the green rayon ribbon, embroider leaves to complete the design.
7. Make up, putting the embroidered velvet on the green damask, and edging the velvet with fine gold cord, and the completed cushion with thick gold cord. The ruched edging is optional.

Velvet and damask are combined with overblown peony roses on this cushion.

Work in progress on Leslie's Rose Dream cushion.

PEONY ROSE CUSHION

This double frilled moiré taffeta cushion is for the romantic at heart. The design is simple, but the technique not for the impatient! We have not specified the exact colours of each rose in the cushion—with your advanced skills we leave you to make those design decisions.

MATERIALS

2m (2¹/₄yds) dusty pink moiré taffeta
1m (1yd, 5in) each of three different shades of
   pink double sided satin ribbon, 1cm
   (¹/₂in) wide
3m (3¹/₂yds) palest pink double sided satin
   ribbon, 2cm (1in) wide
DMC cotton thread:
   pale green

INSTRUCTIONS

1. Cut a 38cm (15in) square of dusty pink moiré taffeta.
2. Make 5 large peony roses in various shades of pink satin ribbon (see Stitch Glossary II).
3. Make 2 small peony roses in two different shades of pink satin ribbon.
4. Make 4 full ribbon roses and 8 rosebuds in various shades of pink (see Stitch Glossary II).
5. Following the diagram, place the peony roses in position on the fabric, the large ones first, then

position the 2 small peony roses. Add the ribbon roses, then the buds. Stitch in place very securely.

6. Referring to the diagram, embroider ribbon leaves and stems to complete the design.

7. Make up the cushion with a very full double frill. The design effect of this cushion relies on the generosity of the fabric.

A double-frilled moiré pillow with delicately-shaded peony roses. (Instructions on page 98.)

A heart-shaped pillow for St Valentine's Day. (Instructions on page 101.)

ST VALENTINE'S ROSE PILLOW

MATERIALS

$1^1/_2$m ($1^3/_4$yds) cream moiré taffeta
2cm (1in) wide double sided satin ribbon:
    pale pink 1., 1m (1yd, 5in)
    pale pink 2., $1^1/_2$m ($1^3/_4$yds)
    deep pink 1., 1m (1yd, 5in)
    deep pink 2., $1^1/_2$m ($1^3/_4$yds)

INSTRUCTIONS

1. Cut a heart shape from the cream moiré taffeta, 33cm x 33cm (13in x 13in) approximately.
2. Make up 3 peony roses (see Stitch Glossary II) in 3 different colours, using a deeper shade of ribbon for the centre of each flower, and a paler ribbon for the outer petals.
3. Stitch the roses to the fabric in a spray shape, as shown in the diagram (not to scale).
4. Make 3 rosebuds, (see Stitch Glossary II). Attach to the fabric according to the diagram, making sure they are very secure.
5. Complete the design by making ribbon leaves and embroidering stem stitch to link the flowers and leaves.
6. Make up a heart pillow with a very generous frill.

♡ PERFECT
PRESENTS

A trio of embroidered lace handkerchiefs. (Instructions on page 106.)

A HAND embroidered gift is one of the most personal and thoughtful presents you can give. In this chapter we suggest a few ideas that can be developed into a whole range of themes. (Of course any of the other projects in this book can be given as a gift!)

Some use the simplest stitches which a beginner can tackle without a qualm, and there are gifts to inspire the experienced embroiderer. Knowing that your time and talent have gone into their making, embroidered presents are guaranteed to give the recipient lasting pleasure.

Once embroidery is a part of your life, the next project is always on your mind—and making a stock of gifts is one way of developing your creative talents. When the Christmas rush is on, you can relax! The presentation of handmade gifts is very important. Choose paper and ribbon to complement the theme of the gift—pastel tissues and narrow ribbons for baby presents, an appropriate box lined with tissue and wrapped with a printed glossy paper for a wedding gift.

THREE HANDKERCHIEFS

Purchase handkerchiefs, with or without lace trimming.

DESIGN 1

For this design, we chose a pure linen handkerchief with hand-rolled edges and drawn thread work.

Following the diagram, embroider three tiny bullion roses, single and double French knots, and leaves in a selection of pastel colours. Link the flowers with stalks in stem stitch and tie a tiny pale pink ribbon bow around the posy.

DESIGN 2

This handkerchief is made from pure cotton with a heavy lace trim.

Make 2 small pink ribbon roses and attach them with white thread to one corner of the handkerchief. Following the diagram, embroider white French knots above and below the roses, and trim with green leaves and stems.

DESIGN 3

This handkerchief is again made from pure cotton, with a fine lace border.

Following the diagram and using pink silk ribbon as yarn, embroider a small rose in rosette stitch, in one corner of the handkerchief. Using this rose as the centrepiece, add 2 ribbon buds on either side. Embroider pink French knots and buds in pastel colours and join with green embroidered stems.

BABY GIFTS

Welcoming a new baby with a personal gift is one of the greatest pleasures, both for the giver and the recipient. These ideas are to inspire you; simple embroidered designs can be added to the most basic of baby clothes to add a touch of style. Singlets, pram covers, sun hats and socks can all be decorated with embroidery.

Here we show you a special dress, a blanket and a matching baby pillow. Starting with the blanket, we used the theme of a heart for each item, suitable for a boy or girl.

BABY BLANKET

This is for experienced embroiderers.

MATERIALS

1 cream woollen satin-bound baby blanket
DMC cotton thread
    cream
    pale apricot   pink 3.
    lemon   lilac
    pale blue   green 1.
    pink 1.   green 2.
    pink 2.   green 3.

$^1/_2$m (20in) pink silk ribbon, 2.5mm ($^1/_8$in) wide

Baby pillow, blanket and dress embroidered in matching motifs.

¹/₂m (20in) cream silk ribbon, 2.5mm (¹/₈in)
   wide
Appleton's wool yarns:
   pink 1.   pale blue
   pink 2.   lilac 1.
   pink 3.   lilac 2.
scraps of fine cord

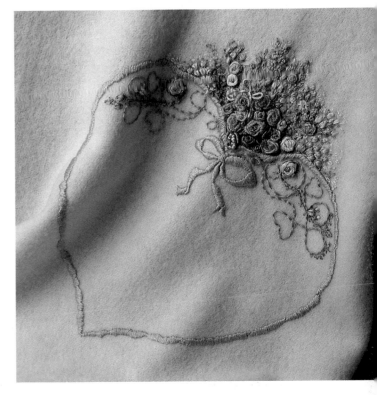

Close-up of baby blanket design.

Instructions

1. Draw a large heart shape in the middle of the blanket.
2. Using a similar method to the bow described for the posy on page 21, tie a bow at the centre of the heart. Satin stitch the heart shape and bow in pale blue cotton, working very loosely.
3. Following the diagram, and starting with bullion roses thickly embroidered in the centre of the top of the heart, fill in the design with flowers and leaves, blending the colours as shown in the photograph.
4. As the design flows outward, make the flowers smaller and more delicate, joining the flowers with stems and leaves.
5. On the inside of the heart, place green cotton thread on a random, flowing pattern (see diagram), tacking down the cotton with tiny stitches to give a soft effect.
6. Add 2 large pink shaded roses using rosette stitch. Finish off with small buds on both edges.
7. *Do not press*—but wrap with love.

Baby Pillow

Materials

1m (1¹/₄yds) fine cream cotton fabric
1m (1¹/₄yds) fine narrow lace trim

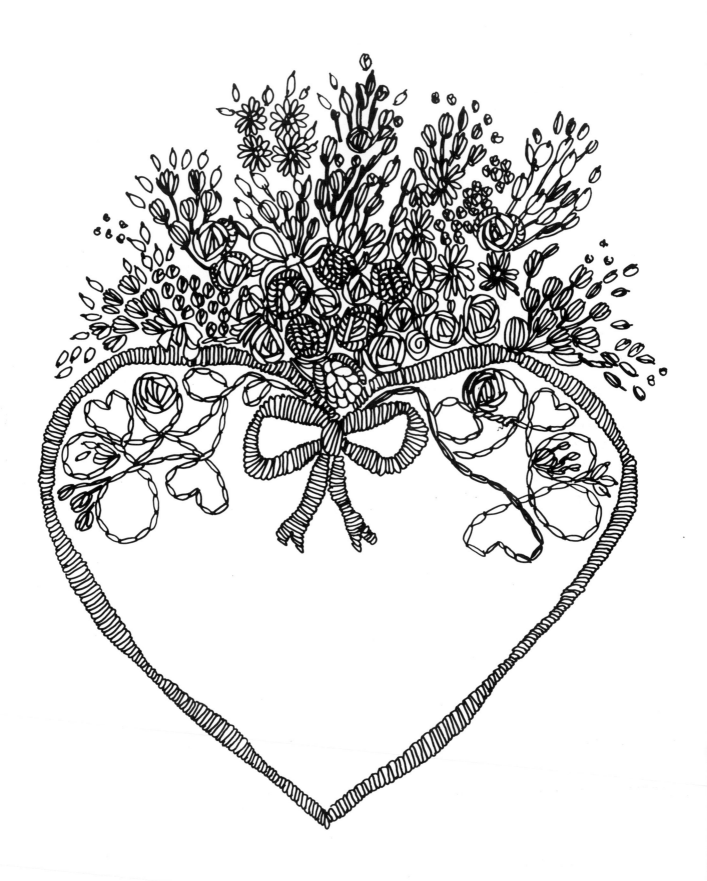

DMC cotton thread:
    pink
    blue
    green

INSTRUCTIONS

1. Cut an oblong of cream cotton fabric 38cm x 27cm (15in x 10in). Draw an oval in the centre of the fabric.
2. Following the diagram, embroider 17 bullion roses using pink cotton yarn. Add tiny green leaves to each rose.
3. In the centre of the oval, draw 4 tiny heart shapes. Embroider around the hearts with bullion stitch in blue yarn.
4. Add one bullion rose to the centre of each heart. Add green leaves.
5. Trim the oval with narrow lace, stitching by hand.
6. Make up the cushion with a finely ruched edge.

BABY DRESS

We bought a very special handmade cotton dress, trimmed with pin tucks, lace and ribbon.

MATERIALS

DMC cotton thread:
    pale blue
    pale pink
    pale green

INSTRUCTIONS

1. Following the diagram, draw a tiny heart in the centre of the yoke, and embroider in bullion stitch, using pale blue cotton yarn.

2. Embroider a bullion rose on the centre of the heart, using pale pink cotton yarn.
3. Add a tiny bullion rose between each pin tuck, and trim with tiny green leaves.

EMBROIDERED COAT HANGER

This coathanger can be made from scraps of fabric. Choose a plain fabric so that the embroidery will stand out. Calico or chintz is ideal—we have used moiré taffeta for this design.

MATERIALS

1 wooden coat hanger
$^1/_4$m (10in) pale apricot moiré taffeta
small amount polyester wadding (for padding)
$2^1/_2$m ($2^3/_4$yds) apricot double sided satin
    ribbon, 1cm ($^1/_2$in) wide
$^1/_2$m (20in) apricot satin ribbon, 5mm ($^1/_4$in)
    wide
DMC cotton yarns:
    deep apricot
    pale apricot
    green

Two embroidered coathangers, one with a lavender bag attached.

INSTRUCTIONS

1. Cut a double piece of moiré taffeta 41cm x 12cm ($16^1/_2$in x 5in), to fit the shape of the hanger.
2. Make 2 apricot peony ribbon roses (see Stitch Glossary II) from double sided ribbon, 1cm ($^1/_2$in) wide, but omit the centre bud. Stitch the roses to the moiré taffeta, following the diagram.
3. Embroider deep apricot French knots at the centre of each peony rose.

4. Following the diagram, embroider bullion roses, buds, French knots and leaves to complete the design.
5. Make up the hanger cover, covering the bottom edge with satin ribbon. Pad with polyester filling and cover the hanger handle with satin ribbon. An additional touch is to attach a tiny ribbon-trimmed moiré taffeta bag containing lavender.

APPENDICES

TEMPLATES

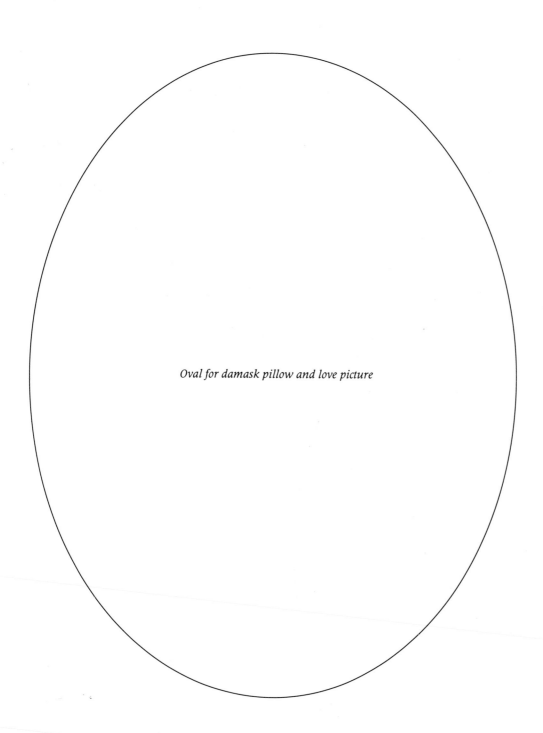

Oval for damask pillow and love picture

Heart for calico cushion and lingerie bag

Oval for yellow moire love cushion

Alphabet

A B C D E F
G H I J K
L M N O P
Q R S T U
V W X Y Z